Samuel Crowther

A Charge Delivered on the Banks of the River Niger in West Africa

Samuel Crowther

A Charge Delivered on the Banks of the River Niger in West Africa

ISBN/EAN: 9783744756327

Printed in Europe, USA, Canada, Australia, Japan

Cover: Foto ©ninafisch / pixelio.de

More available books at **www.hansebooks.com**

A CHARGE

DELIVERED

ON THE BANKS OF THE RIVER NIGER IN

WEST AFRICA.

BY

SAMUEL ADJAI CROWTHER, D.D. OXON.,

(NATIVE MISSIONARY BISHOP).

LONDON:
SEELEY, JACKSON, & HALLIDAY,
54, FLEET STREET.

1866.

LONDON :

PRINTED BY C. F. HODGSON & SON,
GOUGH SQUARE, FLEET STREET, E.C.

CONTENTS.

THE

YORUBA COUNTRY, &c.

with the Course of the

NIGER & TSHADDA.

Throughout the various Yoruba districts (Yoruba Proper, Egba, Egbado, Ijebu, Ijesha, Ekun &c.), the language is identical: the dialectic variations not being greater than between some of our English counties.

Statute Miles.

0	50	100

Church Missionary Stations are underlined, as *Abbeokuta*.

Port of Cameroon

A CHARGE,

&c. &c.

My dear beloved Brethren,—

The object of this meeting, which is the first gathering together of the Bishop and Clergy in this Mission, is, to take a retrospective view of our work in this country; to know what has been done, in what way it has been done; to detect our errors and to correct them, so as to be able to start with fresh vigour and earnestness in the strength of the Lord in this good work. If it be necessary for the army and the navy, the merchants, and others in different departments of labour, to take from time to time a review of the past, to ascertain the state of their staff, the progress of their work, and the healthy state of their funds, so as to enable them to suggest suitable plans for future operations, with a renewed energy and resolute determination to accomplish their objects; —if this is needful in other departments of operations, it is more so with us missionaries, to whom are committed certain talents by the Great Householder, to occupy till He come. In doing which, may the Lord help us to be faithful.

I. A review of the past in this Mission will bring to remembrance many things of a chequered nature, things which will excite in us feelings of pain and regret, which will call forth in us the exercise of implicit faith, and fresh earnestness in prayers and supplications to the God of Missions, and things which will excite feelings of hope and expectation, which will stimulate us to persevering efforts to labour on, believing that though our faith may sometimes be sorely put to the test, yet that in His own good time the Lord will answer our prayers, and grant our earnest, humble petitions, to establish firmly this Mission among the teeming population of the countries through which these mighty rivers flow.

Among the matters of pain and deep regret above alluded to, I may mention the failure of the great efforts which were made by the British Government, and the well-digested plans of Christian philanthropists in England for the welfare of this country, resulting in the Niger Expedition of 1841, presided over by our much lamented late Prince Consort with deepest interest, having in view the twofold object of striking the slave-trade at the root, to introduce industry and legitimate commerce in its place, and of spreading Christianity among the people, as the surest means of elevating Africa in the scale of nations.

One of the greatest projectors and master-minds, who framed the plans of that great enterprise with deep foresight and profound thought, (the late Sir Fowell Buxton,) termed the sum total of that which was needed for the benefit of Africa, the *Gospel* and the *Plough*—in other words, *Christianity* and *Industry*.

These two words are worthy to be written in letters of gold, and preserved in a casket of silver.

Well digested and mature as these plans were, it appeared God's time had not yet come. In the midst of heart-cheering success in the chief object of the Expedition, its progress was arrested by an invisible hand; its successful operations were checked by an unexpected sickness which broke out among the Europeans, on whom solely depended the carrying out the objects of those noble efforts. Being thus beaten back by sickness and painful deaths, in 1842 the Expedition was abandoned, to the great grief of the projectors, and perhaps more so to the great disappointment of the native population, to whom it had held out the highly cherished hopes of their national improvement and prosperity, by having the opportunities of dealing with people of civilized nations, through whose commercial enterprises the natural resources of their countries would be called forth.

This abandonment of the Expedition was a heavy blow to the country. It appeared as if the Niger was doomed to remain in perpetual seclusion, and its mighty waters destined to float down only human cargoes, aggravating the miseries of the country and her people;—as if, instead of becoming a highway through which to convey light, life, and liberty into the heart of the country, it should present as it were an impassable barrier to their introduction, and thus keep the people and country still in the darkness of superstition, ignorance, and vice, in a most servile and abject degradation and slavery, and in a state of spiritual death, in trespasses and sins.

Eleven long and hopeless years rolled away before another effort was made. The heart of the late Mr. McGregor Laird was stirred up. This benevolent English merchant, whom nothing daunted, determined to make another effort, and being backed by Her Majesty's Government, in 1854 he planned out an exploring expedition to the Tshadda branch of the Niger, which proved successful beyond all expectations. Being thus encouraged in 1857 the visit was repeated, with attempts to establish trading stations at given points, where also a Christian Mission was to be commenced among the people. From this period we date the commencement of this Mission. The period from 1842 to 1854 had been indeed a time of severe trial to the faith of God's praying people. He at last answered their prayers, when, in 1857, a beginning was made of a Christian Mission on the banks of the Niger.

The interval between 1857 and this year (1866) has comprised nine years of hopes and fears; yet, being enabled to persevere through many conflicting changes, we have held on, and may well look back and say, "Hitherto the Lord hath helped us."

This review is a necessary preliminary to the special objects for which we this day meet. Such facts teach us God's mysterious dealings with His people; but especially in connection with our work here; so that we may look back and learn resignation to His will, and patiently to wait His good time, when our own fondest hopes are disappointed, and our well-laid plans are frustrated, and to work on in hope, though for a long time we may not see what good may result from our persevering labour, yet believing that God will fulfil His promise, and accomplish His work in His own good time and way.

II. Having thus briefly stated the means God employed to give us a footing in this country, for planting a Christian Mission among the people, it will be necessary for me to describe the commencement of our work; and then to stand as it were upon an eminence, and view the land, and the people, which we have to rescue, and the fortresses and strongholds we have to assail and pull down in our spiritual warfare, under the Captain of our salvation.

Our first station was commenced at Onitsha in 1857, where our dear brother the Rev. J. C. Taylor was landed, assisted by the late Simon Jonas, a Scripture reader. Their lodging was an oblong verandah-hovel, some three feet wide, just enough to spread mats on, without any other comforts. In this place they remained for months, and went out to preach as well as to work, building their own Mission-house on the spot which we now occupy.

The next place attempted to be secured for a Mission-station was Gbebe, at the confluence of the Kwara and Tshadda rivers; which unitedly form the River Niger. While arrangements were being made to effect this, to be completed at my return from the exploring voyage of the Kwara branch, the "Dayspring," the exploring steamer, was wrecked at Jeba, twenty miles above Rabba, where we were obliged to encamp for twelve months. In the meantime, another calamity took place; the trading establishment was accidentally burnt down at Gbebe, and all the property destroyed. It seemed at the time as if another great doom was impending on the working of the Niger, from the wreck of the "Dayspring," and the destruction of the trading establishment at Gbebe; but the God of Missions had something in store for the future of the Niger.

In 1858, the "Sunbeam" was sent for our relief, and some native teachers also to strengthen our hands; thus I was enabled to place three readers, Messrs James Thomas, Edward Klein, and Jacob Newland, to begin at Gbebe; and on the return of Mr. Taylor and Simon Jonas to the coast, to remove their families to the Mission, Mr. John Smart, associated with Mr. W. Romaine, a Christian trader, whose services were secured as a teacher, were left to work the station in Mr. Taylor's absence.

It pleased God to remove Simon Jonas and Edward Klein from our number by death, just at the very time their valuable services seemed to us indispensable. Here again is another mysterious dispensation, too deep for us to fathom.

Akassa station was subsequently taken up, at the mouth of the Nun, with a double view, of having a halting-place at the mouth of the river in going up and down from the upper stations, as well as to do what we can for the people by offering them an opportunity to accept the Gospel of Christ, which is to be preached to all nations.

Death was again permitted to thin our ranks. We were deprived of the valuable services of Mr. James John, Catechist, at Akassa, and of those of Mr. Thomas Joseph, Scripture Reader, at Gbebe.

Last year, 1865, steps were taken to extend our borders; two out-stations were taken up at Onitsha to be worked each by a catechist, under the superintendence of Mr. Taylor. A new station was established at Idda, the capital of Igara, under the superintendence of Mr. Coomber, assisted by two lay teachers. Lokoja, near Gbebe, at the juncture of the Kwara and Tshadda rivers, was occupied under the superintendence of Mr. John, assisted by a lay agent. They labour among a mixed population of Haussa, Nupe, Ekie or Bunu, &c., in the jurisdiction of Mohammedan government, and under their immediate influence.

The situation of Lokoja is on the western side of the Niger, and it is hoped it will become a nucleus of trade; some of the above-mentioned tribes, composing its resident inhabitants, being natives of the countries between the Niger and the coast, this station, if sustained under the protection of our gracious Master, is calculated to extend our operations westward, and to bring the Niger and Yoruba Missions in conjunction at some central point in that direction. While Onitsha and Idda stations promise to work conjointly eastward towards the Tshadda river.

During the same year a Mission was also commenced among the people of Bonny, on the coast in the Bight of Biafra, at present worked by two native teachers, till we can supply it more efficiently. This Mission will ultimately coalesce with that of Onitsha, as the Ibo language is spoken in both places; the vernacular of Bonny is a dialect of the Idzo.

When we look back to the results of these feeble attempts to plant the banner of the cross among our benighted countrymen, and that, too, under many disadvantageous circumstances, one of which has been a want of regular communication and supplies,—though we have not much to speak of, yet we have cause to give thanks unto the Lord of the vineyard, that, under peculiarly trying circumstances, He has not left himself without a witness; His word, preached by faith in His name, has not returned unto Him void; marked changes have been perceptibly observed and felt, and publicly acknowledged both by chiefs and people. The worship of idols is being duly reflected upon by a large number of the population, as far as our influence, or rather the influence of our preaching, has been felt; the system of idol worship is being looked upon by such persons to be of no value, and the fears of receiving injury from their imaginary deities are gradually losing their hold upon the minds of the people. Multitudes have been taught, and many have learned, the value of the only true sacrifice by the blood of our Lord and Saviour Jesus Christ; and in the belief of the efficacy of that blood alone to atone for our sins, many have cast away their idols, and enlisted themselves as candidates of the new religion; and after a due course of regular instruction and careful watch over their characters and motives, believing them to be sincere and in accordance with the requirements of the Gospel, they have been received into the Church by the Sacrament of Baptism; and some have become regular partakers of the Sacrament of the Lord's Supper, in commemoration of His dying love, and to feed on Him by faith.

The statistics of the Mission are exhibited in the following table :—

Stations.	Baptisms.	Candidates.	Communnicants.	School-children.	Congregations.	Marriages.
Onitsha* .	103	23	{ 45 natives { 19 settlers	25	120	8
Idda	—	—	—	24	70†	–
Gbebe ...	39	24	25	{ transferred to Lo- { koja since Gbebe's { destruction by war.		2
Lokoja ...	—	9	—	36	50†	–
Akassa ...	3	—	—	10	22	1
Bonny ...	1	—	—	54	—	–
Total...	146	56	89	149	272	11

III. The effect of the preaching of the Gospel among the heathen authorities and chiefs of the country may thus be estimated. Repeated representations have been made to them of the abominable practice of human sacrifices, which prevail more or less among the different tribes; although the King and chiefs of Onitsha frankly confessed the evil of the thing, yet as they said they could not at once break off from the practice; still, when timely notice was given to the Rev. J. C. Taylor that a human sacrifice was about to take place at such a time, and the evil of the practice was strongly represented to them, they have again and again yielded the "custom," and substituted animal

* The river Niger, near the sea, divides into several branches, of which the Nun is the principal. Akassa is at the mouth of the Nun. Onitsha is 150 miles, Ida 215 miles, and the confluence, Gbebe and Lokoja, 260 miles from the sea.

† The number of persons attending service both at Lokoja and Idda were as high as from 100 to 160; but as these numbers fluctuated, 70 and 50 will be the average attendance at service.

victims in its place. There has been more friendly feelings and union between neighbouring tribes since our establishment among them; and on more than one occasion have the Mission agents been made mediators in reconciling contending parties; and the Mission House has been chosen by themselves as the neutral meeting-ground, and is a place much respected by all.

Industrious habits have been encouraged. When we arrived at Onitsha in 1857, we found the people in a state of idleness, and with its attendant evils; they were scantily and filthily clothed, and in a state bordering upon starvation, especially between the cessation of the old and the ripeness of the new crops: the old crops were barely sufficient to supply their scanty wants for nine months of the year; they did not grow more, although the exuberant fertile soil was ready to yield them a hundredfold increase in return; the remaining three months was a time of dearth and scarcity, when they had to live upon fruits and other edible plants, the spontaneous produce of the fields, as might be found in the bushes anywhere. But since the introduction of the Cassada plants into the country by Mr. Taylor, and other fruit trees, and the people have been taught to raise a second crop of Indian corn by Mr. John Smart, a Scripture reader, and how to grow their yams better by the united example of all the Mission agents, they have had enough to eat and to spare. The introduction of the Cassada plants into the country is universally acknowledged as one of the greatest temporal blessings brought to them by their zealous minister. The trading establishment has contributed greatly to stimulate them to labour in collecting palm oil for sale, for which they are paid in Manchester goods; and now they are getting into the habit of going about more cleanly and decently apparelled.

I regard industry as a necessary, though a secondary, part of missionary labours; it is a direct command of the Apostle Paul to the converts at Thessalonica. "For even when we were with you, this we commanded you, that if any would not work, neither should he eat. For we hear that there are some which walk among you disorderly, not working at all, but are busybodies. Now them that are such we command and exhort by our Lord Jesus Christ, that with quietness they work, and eat their own bread." (2 Thes. iii. 10—12.) Those who were already made converts are commanded and urged to habits of industry. I have enlarged upon this head thus much, to show that we have acted consistently with our profession, by introducing the Gospel and the Plough, or Christianity and Industry; both have worked hand in hand,—the Gospel primarily; Industry, as the handmaid to the Gospel.

But in these days it is necessary to guard such a statement as I have now made from being misinterpreted. Beware of those who propose to suspend, at the beginning, teaching the people by preaching, and first to teach them mechanical arts and industrial habits, to better their temporal condition; and then afterwards to introduce Christianity among the people as a secondary thing: then, say these men of reason, the heathens will believe your preaching, because they will say, these men, who have taught us to make our houses better, to cultivate our lands, and to better our temporal condition, must be true in what they tell us of their new religion. I have been positively told by one of these reasonable advisers, that unless I put aside teaching the natives the art of reading and writing, and teach them carpentry, coopery, cookery, &c., he would never subscribe a farthing towards my missionary work to convert the heathen.

But, my dear brethren, to set aside these futile reasonings, we need not go so far as to the Chinese or to the Hindoos in the East, who have been notable for ages for skill in works of arts, or for a state of affluence, and who are not behind in the literature of the East. Let us look at home, and make our advisers themselves our witnesses, who not only have the honour of being the sons of the first nation in the world, the country which is the seat of wealth, and of arts and sciences, in their present perfection; but also the sons of the nation which is the mainspring of the world, through her wealth, putting all in motion, both by land and water, through the invention of steam, and who can communicate their minds from one country to another with the quickness of the lightning through electricity; surely our advisers cannot deny this wonderful pre-eminence attained by their nation above all others. Let us ask them what favourable effects have these wonderful advantages had upon their own minds towards their reception of the Gospel? Do they so much as pay the smallest honest tribute to the Bible, and the religion which it teaches as being the *source* from which all these blessings flow? I fear there are no such effects. Neither themselves, nor many who maintain such an opinion, are found near the doors of the places where the Gospel is preached: it is to them foolishness. Would their plan be more favourable among the heathens? Painful experience belies this.

The weapons of our warfare are not carnal, but mighty through God to the pulling down of strongholds; it is the faithful preaching of the Gospel, which is the power of God unto salvation to every one that believeth; it is that alone which can work a change in *hearts* both at home and abroad.

IV. Our next enquiry shall be as to the best mode of proceeding in preaching the Gospel among the heathen.

In this we have the best example ever given on the subject, and that by the preaching of Christ himself. The Sermon on the Mount; His Parables; His Discourses; these are the standards of Missionary sermons among the untutored heathen. Take any portion of these, sublime and lofty as the sentiments therein expressed are; yet they are so simple, that every heathen can understand them; and so appropriate, that every one can see himself represented in them. Imitate Christ, then, to reach the understanding, and not to move the feelings only; speak to the people as they are able to bear it; speak to them with all simplicity as to children; a simple exposition and application of a discourse or parable will often be followed by lasting impressions and great effects. In this way I have not only got an attentive hearing from the heathen, but from Mahometans also; bigoted as they are, they could not help attesting to the soundness of the doctrine of our religion, though they could not embrace Christianity lest they should be cast out of the Mosque.

Whether we hope to make converts from among the heathen, or from the followers of Mahomet, our aim should always be to preach to all as to needy and helpless sinners, who must be pardoned through the atoning blood of Christ alone. Preach without a prejudiced mind; the hearts into which the seed is sown belong to the Lord, who owns both the seed and the hearts. The growth of the seed cast into such a heart is in His power, just as we sow our natural seed, both morning and evening, and know not whether this or that shall prosper, or whether both should be alike good. So must we preach the Gospel to a mixed congregation of heathen and Mahometans; thus sowing by prayer and faith, we must leave the results to the Disposer of all hearts, who can influence them by the inspiration of His holy Spirit.

Again, in preaching, divest yourself of a disposition to dispute with Mahometans, or to censure heathens; rather be possessed with the feelings of sympathy with all classes of hearers. Whenever there is an opportunity of preaching to, or speaking with, Mahometans, unfold the truth of the Gospel of Christ in its fulness, commending the truth to their consciences in the sight of God. It was not always that Christ made severe rebukes upon the Scribes and Pharisees, as hypocrites, in His discourses; though some were probably always present to hear Him, though not with the intention to profit, but to watch and catch something from His mouth, that they might accuse Him. Though He knew this, yet generally He preached as if He knew not their wicked intentions. The effects on them we are told thus: " Among the chief rulers, also, many believed on Him, but because of the Pharisees they did not confess Him, lest they should be put out of the synagogue, for they love the praise of men more than the praise of God." Even the officers who were sent on one occasion to apprehend Him, were disarmed by His powerful and resistless preaching, and returned without Him, with this conviction and frank confession of His heart-searching sermon: " Never man spake like this man." Aim at supplying the hearts of the hearers with the infallible truth of the Gospel of Christ, in the room of the doctrines and commandments of men.

With the heathen population we have mostly and chiefly to do: them you must not censure as ignorant, stupid, and foolish idolators; your dealing with them must be that of sympathy and love, as you would deal with the blind who errs out of the way; surely he would not have wittingly gone out of the way, but for want of sight. Thus the Bible tells us, " He" (Satan) " hath shut their eyes that they cannot see, and their hearts, that they cannot understand."

This is beautifully paraphrased by the late celebrated Bishop Heber:—

> " The heathen in their blindness,
> Bow down to wood and stone."

When we first introduce the Gospel to any people,

we should take advantage of any principles which they themselves admit. Thus, though the heathen in this part of Africa possess no written legends, yet wherever we turn our eyes we find among them, in their animal sacrifices, a text which is the mainspring of the Christian faith : " Without shedding of blood there is no remission." Therefore we may with propriety say, "That which ye ignorantly practise declare we unto you :" " The blood of Jesus Christ, the Son of God, cleanseth from all sin."

Whoever observes the rite of animal sacrifices as performed by the heathens in this country, cannot but be struck with the similarity, in many cases, though rudely done, with the Levitical institution. For instance, the application of the blood of the victims on the person of the offerer, or on his forehead, with a tuft of the hair of the beast, or feathers of the bird, most frequently of the pigeon, attached to the blood on the forehead, which must remain on him till it dries and falls off : the application of the blood on the doors and door-posts, and on the lintels : the share of the priests : and the parts which must be taken out into the highway, to be exposed to the evil spirits intended to be pacified or propitiated, reminding one especially of the portion of the burnt-offering, whose ashes must be conveyed to some place without the camp ; and, as we have lately discovered at Onitsha, the yearly human sacrifice for the sin of the nation. All these cannot but lead one back to conclude that these rites must have their remote origin from imitation of the Levitical institution of sacrifices, which have degenerated as they were handed down from the tradition of the Fathers.

Here is a foundation for our preaching. The institution of sacrifices by God as types and shadows of good things to come, will naturally form a grand topic of the doctrine of the Gospel we bring among them.

We admit that it is judicious to introduce at the first among the people such portions of God's word as are necessary for their salvation, such as the Gospels and the historical books of the Old Testament, and, as they are growing in knowledge, the Epistles; yet we do not think, as some would recommend, to withhold from them such parts of the Pentateuch as seem to countenance sacrifices, polygamy, holding of slaves, and other practices, against which we preach as inconsistent with the Christian profession.' The very fact of proving from the Pentateuch the Divine institution of sacrifices, and for what end, will tend to bring home our preaching against their present practices more powerfully to their consciences than otherwise. This is also applicable to the system of polygamy and slave-holding. The honesty of presenting the Holy Scriptures, in all their parts, as God has delivered them to us, will draw more blessing upon our work than keeping back portions of them for fear of defeating our own object. We have no such apprehension. Inasmuch as we have not followed cunningly devised fables, it is our bounden duty to deal honestly with the people committed to our instruction, by not shunning to declare unto them the whole counsel of God; although we are not unmindful that babes must first be nursed with the sincere milk of the word, that they may grow thereby, reserving the strong meats till they are of full age.

By this mode of proceeding the Gospel has been introduced into this part of Africa, and the formidable hindrances have been overcome. I have stated it as a matter of fact, that converts have been made from among the heathen by our preaching. Sometimes, indeed, we have feared and doubted whether some of them were sincere, and knew enough how much would be required of them in their profession of the Christian faith. It was our duty to receive them, as they offered themselves as candidates of the new religion, and to teach them by degrees the principles of Christianity; though with mingled hopes and fears whether they would be able to endure the voyage in which they had embarked. We have discovered, with sorrow and disappointment, that some have only followed for the sake of imagined loaves and fishes to be obtained, and when disappointed would walk no more with us; and some have made shipwreck of their faith from long old habits, which they could not altogether part with and entirely forsake; and others have proved, like Demas, to love this present world: for all these characters are represented among our converts. Yet, by the grace of God, we have been encouraged, by seeing many sincere converts who hold fast their Christian profession without wavering, who seem to be made partakers of Christ, holding the beginning of their confidence steadfast to the end.

V. The antagonists of modern Christian Missionary Societies sometimes strive to discredit our work by saying that the present system of teaching Christianity to the heathen must be defective, because it has not been followed by a Pentecostal success.

To this I reply, that the introduction of Christianity among the natives of West Africa is beset with many and great disadvantages, one of which is, the want of a written language. Putting aside the means God was pleased at the first to use, to aid the Apostles in propagating the new faith,—such as the miraculous gift of tongues, the gift of miracles and of healings, &c., as credentials of their Divine mission, —it was a great advantage that the age in which Christianity was introduced into the world was that of literature. The Greeks and Romans, who were successively masters of the then known world, were men of letters; their literary works, though heathen productions, have continued to be the standard of academical honours and degrees, to modern Christian scholars. To the Jews were committed the oracles of God. If this be true, here were natural facilities in the way of the Apostles in prosecuting their important mission among both Jews and Gentiles. St. Paul, in his first sermon at Athens, could bring to the remembrance of his sophistical and sceptical hearers the saying of one of their standing authorities, a poet who said, "We are also His offspring." So St. Peter took advantage to refer the Cretans to the saying of one of them, who said, "The Cretans are always liars, evil beasts, slow bellies." The Thessalonians and the Bereans were particularly noted in that they searched the Scriptures daily to see whether those things were so. Here at once were the advantages of literature; it enabled the people to search and prove for themselves, out of the Scriptures, the veracity of the word preached. We learn also that many who used curious arts, imposed upon the people by means of books; for, on proving the veracity of the Scriptures, they brought their books together, and burned them before all men. And they counted the price of them, and found it fifty thousand pieces of silver. Christian Missionaries to this part of Africa have never had the advantage of books or a reading people. Their disadvantages in this respect are two-fold; not only that the natives, whom they come out to teach, have not a written language, but that the Missionaries themselves must make a written language out of the lips of the natives, learn the language, and then teach the use of it to them in books. Thus, with the introduction of Christianity, they have also to introduce the elements of literature, before they can expect any amount of results in the Missionary work by the reading of God's word.

This great drawback must be gradually overcome by a steady and persevering labour in places where we have to establish new Missions. Where this great difficulty has been overcome, the hitherto ignorant natives, who had never known how to derive information from the thoughts of others through the medium of books, nor how to communicate their own thoughts to others through that channel, have betaken themselves, with all diligence, to acquire the art of reading; and it may be witnessed in those who have mastered this new and mysterious acquirement, what is their estimate of the art of reading, by their attachment to the portions of God's holy word translated into their native tongue, which they value as a pearl of great price. They, having nothing here like the Vedas of the Hindoos from which to argue for the antiquity of their mythology, and nothing like the Koran of the Mahometans to stiffen them in arguing for the superiority of the religion of Mahomet to that of Christ, receive the translated portions of the Bible which we put into their hands, with the eagerness and simplicity of children, even the engrafted word which is able to save their souls. Thus God is overruling the very great obstacle in the way of the rapid progress of Christian missions, wherever it has been overcome by persevering labour and faith, to a permanent establishment of the knowledge of His Gospel among the heathen.

Idolatrous worship, with all its concomitant evils, which is repugnant to the spread of Christianity, is another great obstacle to be contended with. But this is common to all heathen nations and countries in the world.

Another great evil with which we have to contend in this country is the system of polygamy. It is indeed a great obstacle, but it may be overcome. Many would place it prominently above all other obstacles in the way of Christian Missionaries in Africa; but perhaps I do not go to the same extent as they do in ranking it as the greatest hindrance in the way of the heathen embracing Christianity, though it is the most common. The system prevails throughout the country; it insinuates itself into the corrupt and unsubdued will of the children of Adam; it has become a second nature; to break off from it is to part with the right eye, the right hand, or the right foot; it is such a darling system to depraved nature, that it does not only enslave the practisers of it themselves, but it presses thousands of unwilling victims into its service. So the song of the women of Israel in honour of David after his successive victories over the Philistines may well be applied to this system:— "Saul hath slain his thousands, and David his ten thousands." Other obstacles, taken separately, have kept back, each its thousands, but the system of polygamy its ten thousands. The system is a *net* of the *lust* of the *flesh*, which is the parent evil. "It is the fault and corruption of the nature of every man, that is naturally engendered of the offspring of Adam; whereby man is very far gone from original righteousness, and is of his own nature inclined to evil, so that the flesh lusteth always contrary to the spirit." But when once the old man is crucified, the meshes of polygamy will give way, and the wrongly oppressed victims enclosed therein will easily be set at liberty and the system abolished. "For the law of the Spirit of life in Christ Jesus hath made me free from the law of sin and death." Rom. viii. 2.

But as some have, in this day, advocated the admission of polygamists into the Christian Church, let us honestly view this subject in its various bearings, and enquire into the lawfulness and unlawfulness of the system from God's own word and acts, and from its effects upon our social state and happiness.

The act of God, co-existent with the Creation, is to be taken as the standard pattern throughout the family of mankind. "It is not good that the man should be alone; I will make him an helpmeet for him." "And the rib which the Lord God had taken from the man made he a woman, and brought her unto the man. And Adam said, This is now bone of my bones and flesh of my flesh : she shall be called Woman, because she was taken out of man. Therefore shall a man leave his father and his mother, and shall cleave unto his wife; and they shall be one flesh." This was God's first act in our social state, the man and his wife. And to this the last of the Prophets refers (Mal. ii. 14, 15): "Did He not make one? Yet had he the residue of the Spirit. And wherefore one? That He might seek a goodly seed. Therefore take heed to your spirit, and let none deal treacherously with the wife of his youth."

Our Saviour confirmed this ordinance, when He said to His disciples, "Have ye not read, that He which made them at the beginning, made them male and female; and said, For this cause shall a man leave father and mother, and shall cleave unto his wife; and they twain shall be one flesh. Wherefore they are no more twain, but one flesh."

The Apostle St. Paul was very clear in this respect in his Epistle to the Corinthians : "Let every man have his own wife, and let every woman have her own husband."

After the lapse of 1600 years from the Creation, and Adam's fall, when mankind had departed from the original institution, and God saw fit in His righteous judgment to punish the world of the ungodly, he restored out of the ruins of man's depravity that holy estate which had been buried in the rubbish of corruption, in honour of his own original institution, from which man had departed, by saving eight persons, *four pairs*, four men and four women, from the waters of the flood. If God was not pleased to create Adam more helps-meet for him than one at the creation,—had it been His will that the system of polygamy should be introduced, maintained, and encouraged in the world,—how easy it was for Him to save several innocent young females, who had not participated in the wickedness of their parents, that by them the earth might again be quickly repeopled? What did God mean to show to those who come after, but that He still regarded and honoured His first ordinance, " very good," by this divine testimony in the midst of His fierce anger, when He drowned the world of the ungodly?

But this was not heeded. Like other evils, polygamy has extended to remote nations and to succeeding ages. But what are its consequences? It has enslaved the female population of the countries where it prevails, and made many to be miserable victims to the carnal lust and depraved appetite of one man. It has wrenched from them the right of nature which God has implanted in each for her own social happiness. Let us stand above the level, and take a view of this social evil. We are in the midst of it, and are in no danger of misrepresentation. When a man has commenced the life of a polygamist, he at the same time has commenced a life of neglect of conjugal duty and disquietude; the neglect creates quarrel, and disturbance of domestic peace ensues. It is impos-

sible for every polygamist in this country to support
from two to half a dozen wives out of his own scanty
resources; and when this is the case, there is no alter-
native but that every wife must enter into a life of
labour and drudgery, and shift for herself the best
way she can; hence, to earn her livelihood, she must
become a carrier of loads from one market town to
another, or she must become a trader to neighbouring
towns and tribes, which involves an absence of days,
and weeks, and months, from home; and on her return,
it has not unfrequently happened, that she provides
for the husband out of her earnings, in addition to
providing for herself and her children, if she has
any; for the chief care of the children devolves
on the mother and her relatives. The occasional
gift of a few cowries from the father to the children
for their morning gruel, and perhaps occasional
share of yams to the mother, constitute, mainly,
the support from the father. The mother, having
the chief maintenance of the children in many
tribes, the native law has justly decided that she
has more right in the children than the father,
though he exercises authority over all. It has been
often remarked by the men themselves, that when a
man had but one wife, there was that degree of love
and affection between them as might be observed in a
married state in civilized countries; they were one in
everything. But no sooner was a second wife added,
than the cord of union and affection was broken, and
domestic evils immediately showed themselves. Hence
arose this memorable proverb among the Yoruba
females, *Obiri kò rubo ki o li orogun,* "No woman

would ever undergo the expenses of a sacrifice, to procure a rival," (*i. e.*, that her husband may have an additional wife). These are the feelings of the female population on the subject; the proverb is their own, it is their watch-word, showing the repugnance of their feelings against the system, and may be heard among them to-day; but it is generally suppressed, like their other proper rights, which they forego, for fear of being reproached with jealousy.

There is another very cruel oppression practised under this system, as it may be observed in this country; that is, the practice of a walled harem; a large open courtyard, like that of a prison, is walled up, wherein scores of unfortunate females are shut up,* being the wives of a king, or chief. What is told of these unfortunate persons rather excites pity than reproach. They are reasonable beings, in whom God has planted certain rights and feelings in common with other people; but when such rights are selfishly taken away from them, and those feelings cruelly oppressed, are not their cruel and sensual oppressors more to be blamed than they? Can it be otherwise expected but that these unfortunate, despairing prisoners, enslaved to the lust and carnal appetite of a person old enough, it may be, to be their grandfather, should scale the walls at night, at the risk of their being detected by the keepers of the women, and severely

---

* N.B. To beguile the tedious hours of seclusion from public exercises within these walls, the time of these unfortunate persons is employed in spinning cotton wool into thread, or dying cotton cloths in indigo blue, the proceeds of which add to their maintenance.

punished, or even of losing their heads for it. Selfishness has disturbed the equilibrium of social rights, there being as many young men who are also thus selfishly deprived of their right of the social privilege of an allotted companion.

One evil leads to another; for the safe keeping of the harem, numbers of eunuchs are made to be keepers of the women.

The system of polygamy will not check the evil of sensuality, or else we would not have occasion so often to witness the accusation of one polygamist against another polygamist for intrusion into his right. And if the system be such as it has been stated, whether we look at it on the one hand from the personal wrong done to the female sex, or on the other hand the injustice and oppression of which the man is guilty, who, I may ask, correctly knowing this state of things, can conscientiously recommend its continuance?

It has been suggested by some, that the present polygamists could be received into the Church by the Sacrament of Baptism, on the condition that such persons promise not to add to their already possessed wives; but who can guarantee that young persons will not purposely hold back till they have possessed as many wives as their hearts desire, before they offer themselves to be admitted into the Church by the same rite after the example of their fathers? The human heart is so deceitful and desperately wicked, that it will ever find a loophole to gratify its carnal propensity. Once establish a precedent, you cannot easily change it.

Having adverted to the system of polygamy as being a great hindrance in the way of the male population to embrace Christianity, it remains also to ask, What hinders the female population from a readier profession of the religion? Whether their husbands be polygamists or not, as long as a woman remains faithful to her husband, upon her profession of faith in Christ as the all-sufficient Saviour of sinners, after a course of instruction, she is received into the Church by baptism: her husband's fault cannot be imputed to her; and if her will were consulted, she would rather be the only help-meet for him.

As one half of the population of any village, town, or country is composed of females, it might be thought that the number of female converts would double or triple that of the males, many of whom are prevented from coming forward, being polygamists. It might have been so if there were not other obstacles in the way; there might have been no difficulty, comparatively speaking, in making the female population converts to Christianity. Yet with some advantages in their favour, we find in many cases that the females have proved not quite so easily brought round to embrace Christianity as might have been expected. They are the mot addicted to idolatrous worship; their combination with their priestesses is a formidable barrier to break through; they have such a tenacious influence over one another as defies any other power, but that of the irresistible influence of the Spirit of God to detach them from it, so that we are sometimes almost in despair of ever being able to do any good among them.

Grandmothers and mothers have been found to prove a great hindrance in the way of their children or family connections coming forward to embrace Christianity. These influential grandams who could say, " After I am waxed old, shall I have pleasure," are the very ones who, like their companions of the other sex, stand aloof from Christianity as interfering with the custom of their ancestors. They have been born in idolatry, brought up in it, have a most superstitious belief in it ; they are wedded to it, and in it they determine to die, and go to the generation of their fathers.

We have thus considered what are the chief hindrances in the way of the reception of Christianity both by males and females ; polygamy on the part of the males, and superstitious idolatry on the part of the females. But neither the one nor the other is the sole cause or *root* of the evil. The great evil is the universal one which prevails in countries where the Gospel has been long preached, as well as in heathen lands where it is recently introduced. The secret of all is this, " the carnal mind is enmity against God ; for it is not subject to the law of God, neither indeed can be." It is the corrupt will of man, which will not submit to the law of God : the doctrine of repentance, and amendment of life, and mortification of the flesh, is what the proud rebellious heart will not so soon yield obedience to. When the will is subdued, every other obstacle gives way with it. The polygamists very soon see their mistake in their way of life contrary to the ordinance of God in the holy estate of matrimony ; they will soon see rightly their own true interest, and their duty to their neighbours. When once they have a correct view of this, they give themselves no rest till they reform. They are never compelled to do anything; we leave the matter to their own deliberate consideration; they are never urged to cast away their idolatrous objects of worship; but they either voluntarily cast them away themselves, or bring them to us, being truly convinced of their utter helplessness. Thus we find the most obstinate rebels against truth and the Gospel, who at first were staunch opponents to Christianity, become zealous followers of the Lord Jesus Christ by faith in His blood, both men and women.

We might have dwelt on Mahometanism as another obstacle in the way of Christianity; but it is so well known, that it is unnecessary to say a word about it. Yet I may notice some devices they practise in this country to recommend its adoption to the heathens. They pursue systems in direct opposition to Christian missionaries. Besides propagating their religion with the sword, they work upon the super-stition of the heathen by making charms, which they sell to them to confide in like their own idolatrous fetishes or greegrees. These charms, which are writings of words or sentences in Arabic from the Koran, are made to suit almost all occasions, and the superstitious wishes of the people. I may mention some, as follows:—*Protective charms.* These are made to protect against every danger, at home or abroad, against sickness, witchcraft, an evil eye; but especially when they go to war or on kidnapping expe-ditions, to ward off arrows or gunshot, and to make blunt the edge of the sword if they come to close contact with their antagonists in battle.—*Vanishing charms.* These are issued to a warrior or kidnapper, that he might disappear and vanish away when he is in danger of being caught himself in his slave-hunting raid.—*Successful charms.* These are issued to a person that he may have a good luck in any under-taking; to catch slaves in war, to succeed in anything taken in hand, to prosper in trade or on a journey; to obtain favour in the sight of the rich or great, or of any one it is sought; to make one rich, &c.—*Pro-creative charms.* These are mostly sought for by women who are very anxious to be favoured with children; and in case of conception, as it is believed through such influences, the infant is destined to be a Mahometan. Thus, if there be one thousand births under such a delusion, one thousand infants are converted to Mahometanism by means of charms. When such a child is grown up, preach to him a change of religion, his reply will be, "I cannot, I was destined to be born a Mahometan."—*Confounding charms,* which are often called tying charms; because it is believed that such charms have an enchanting and fascinating influence on the person against whom they are issued, that he cannot act in opposition to that influence. Thus, to tie or confound the enemies with whom they are at war, they throw or secretly bury such charms in their camp or town, and thus the people are led to believe that the enemies will be con-founded or paralysed. Charms are issued out against any person of property, or in better circumstances, whose prosperity is envied, that he may become

a spendthrift and waster, and be reduced to poverty·
Charms are given to render a man an idiot, charms to
kill, &c. &c. In short, there is not a case for which
the superstitious, credulous heathen apply to a Mahometan priest, for which he does not procure
him a charm. Can we be surprised that the foolish
heathen, who are thus worked upon by a man looking
into a book and writing out such scraps from it in
the name of God and Mahomet his prophet, are more
easily made converts to Mahometanism than to
Christianity? But Christian Missionaries cannot
have recourse to such deceits to recommend the way
of salvation to the heathen.

Foolish, however, as the heathen are to believe in
these things, yet the popular feelings are, and their
belief is this, and they have often expressed it, that
the religion of the Anazora (i. e., Christianity) will
supersede all other religions in the end.

VI. Before I conclude I must touch on the subject
of occupying new Stations.

Small and insignificant as it may appear to be, yet
we must regard the occupation of a new Station as a
step onward in extending the Redeemer's kingdom.
Christ sent his disciples to every city and place
whither he himself would come, to preach the Gospel.
Not only the conversion of souls in such a place or
village is of the utmost importance; but God may
make such a place another starting point to occupy
new ground, or to work wider around that locality.

Yet great caution is required at the occupation of a
new Station. It is necessary, according to the custom
of the country, to exchange presents, and to give

presents, which is another name for paying for land, by which our right to occupy it unmolested is recognized. These preliminary precautions are prudent and necessary; yet it is right, at the same time, that we do not impose upon ourselves the unnecessary tax of giving periodically, so that it should become an established rule, from which we may find it difficult afterwards to free ourselves. We should not forget the cupidity and selfishness of some native chiefs, whose aim and desire is to make a gain of us by constantly drawing from our imagined inexhaustible resources as much as they can; this is a particular trait in their character. We should never be backward to impress on them that it is their duty to bear a part share in the expenses of the Mission from the very beginning, till they are able to bear the whole cost themselves.

The principle of self-support should never be lost sight of. To introduce this system, the plan of a Christian relief fund may be set on foot, which must be gradually improved upon, bearing in mind the principle of contributing to the expenses of the Mission, and ultimately of self-support in due time.

VII. Before I bring this Charge to a close, there is another topic which is frequently brought to my notice, with a view to perplex, not to satisfy doubts. The question is, What shall become of the heathens who die without having the opportunity of hearing the Gospel of Jesus Christ? This is a new version of the question of the inquisitive hearer in the Gospel: "Lord, are there few that be saved?" To such captious questions our answer is furnished by St. Paul, Rom. ii. 11—16: "For there is no respect of persons with God. For as many as have sinned without law shall also perish without law: and as many as have sinned in the law shall be judged by the law. For not the hearers of the law are just before God, but the doers of the law shall be justified. For when the Gentiles, which have not the law, do by nature the things contained in the law, these, having not the law, are a law unto themselves; which shew the work of the law written in their hearts, their conscience also bearing witness, and their thoughts the meanwhile accusing, or else excusing, one another. In the day when God shall judge the secrets of men, by Jesus Christ, according to my Gospel." This should be a sufficient reply to such a question.

With all submission, I will remark that it is not the will of God to reveal unto us what shall become of such persons.

Known unto Him are all His works from the creation of the world. "The secret things belong unto the Lord our God, but those things which are revealed belong unto us and to our children for ever and ever, that we may do all the works of this law." Our duty is plain,—"Go ye therefore and teach all nations." Although eighteen hundred years have elapsed since this command was given, and the Gospel is not yet universally preached to all nations, yet still the command continues in full force,—"Go and teach all nations."

Though we are not permitted to know what shall become of those who have not had the opportunity to hear of the Gospel of Christ, yet we are plainly told by Christ himself what shall become of those who hear of Him, but believe not. "They are condemned already, because they believe not in the name of the only-begotten Son of God: and this is the condemnation, that light is come into the world, but men love darkness rather than light, because their deeds are evil."

Hence, the servant that knoweth his master's will, and doeth it not, shall be beaten with many stripes; but he that knoweth not, and doeth things worthy of stripes, shall be beaten with few stripes.

To the inquisitive inquirer of what shall become of the heathens who have not had the opportunity of hearing of the Gospel of Christ, this is the answer: Thou who knowest thy master's will, but doest it not, shall be beaten with many stripes, in proportion to your light, knowledge, and opportunity you have, but which you have abused. The heathens, who have not the like opportunity of knowing, but commit things worthy of stripes, shall be beaten with few stripes, in proportion to their lack of additional knowledge and light. "Shall not the judge of all the earth do right?"

S. A. CROWTHER,

Missionary Bishop.

Appendix.

[*Appeal issued in* 1864.]

WEST-AFRICAN NATIVE BISHOPRIC FUND.

THE REV. SAMUEL CROWTHER, D.D.,* has been consecrated Bishop of those parts of West Africa which lie beyond the limits of the Diocese of Sierra Leone. He has received the degree of D.D. from the University of Oxford, and was consecrated on the 29th of June by the Archbishop of Canterbury. This appointment marks an era which is full of hope for the extension of Christianity in those regions by a Native Church under a Native Episcopacy. Dr. Crowther will still continue in connexion with the Church Missionary Society, receiving his salary from its funds, communicating with its Secretaries, and acting in concurrence with the Society in all Missionary operations in which the Missionaries of the Society are engaged.

But, beyond those operations, a Native Bishop will have large opportunities of stimulating native zeal, if he have the means of making small grants out of a fund at his own disposal, as a commencement and encouragement of local Missionary efforts. For example, he may prompt native converts to erect preaching-houses or school-houses by offers of comparatively trifling pecuniary aid. He will be able to meet cases in which Native Chiefs, not yet converted to Christi-

---

* Dr. Crowther was born of heathen parents, in the town of Oshogun, in West Africa. He was taken prisoner by a hostile tribe, and sold as a slave. He was afterwards rescued by a British cruiser, and liberated, and educated in Sierra Leone.

anity, apply to Missionaries to send them Teachers or School-masters, who will be ready partly to support them, if their first expenses and a portion of their salary be defrayed. Ho will be able to receive messengers from distant Kings and Tribes, who occasionally visit a Mission station, and whom it is desirable to entertain as guests. He may engage inter-preters and copyists in reducing new languages. In such and many similar cases, if the funds of the society were em-ployed, there would be danger of checking that spirit of self-reliance and independent action which it is most desirable to cherish in the Native Church, while to many such objects the funds of the Society are not applicable.

If the African Native Bishopric fulfils, through the blessing of the great Head of the Church, the expectations which may be reasonably entertained, there will be a constant and in-creasing call upon the fund from year to year, as the Native Church extends its bounds. It will soon require its own Theological School, and a Native Church Fund. In this prospect the contributions now received will be husbanded with all due caution; but it is hoped that, when they are ex-hausted, the appeal may be renewed. For whatever is con-tributed through this channel will tend to foster the free action and self-support of the Native Church, instead of an unhealthy dependence upon, and subordination to, a foreign Missionary Society. As the objects to which the fund is applicable in-crease in numbers and importance, the Bishop will take counsel with his Native Presbyters respecting its distribution.

The Bishop's Fund might be further applied with ad-vantage in occasionally redeeming Christian converts who have been carried into captivity, in promoting native industry by the gift of cotton gins or mechanical tools, and for other presents to Chiefs; for which purposes the funds of the Church Missionary Society cannot properly be employed.

There will also be at first many extra personal expenses, such as an outfit, and, afterwards, journeys and voyages, for which the fund will be available.

It is the Bishop's wish that all Contributions to this Fund should be paid into the hands of the Treasurers in London, with whom he proposes to communicate from time to time as to the appropriation of the Fund, and to whom he will transmit an annual account of the expenditure, and notices of the Missionary operations which it has helped to sustain.

Out of this Fund the Mission in Bonny has been supported, the native chiefs having been induced to contribute half the expense of the buildings. Encouragement to industry is also a charge upon this Fund. A statement of the receipts and expenditure is to be had on application to the Church Missionary House.

Treasurers of the Fund, JOHN GURNEY HOARE, Esq., T. FOWELL BUXTON, Esq., and the Rev. HENRY VENN. Contributions to be paid to the "West-African Native Bishopric Fund," Messrs. BARNETT, HOARE, and Co., Bankers, Lombard Street, City, E.C.

London: Printed by C. F Hodgson and Son, Gough Square, Fleet Street.

www.ingramcontent.com/pod-product-compliance
Lightning Source LLC
Chambersburg PA
CBHW021441090426
42739CB00009B/1578